This book belongs to

_____

Islamic Nursery Rhymes

Revised Edition

Published by Mindworks Publishing 2016

Copyright © 2016 Mindworks Publishing and Elizabeth Lymer

Mindworks Publishing,
Missouri City,
TX 77489

mindworkspublishing@gmail.com

First published by Greenbird Publishing 2013

Text ©Elizabeth Lymer 2013
Illustrations © Fatimah De Vaux Davies 2013

All rights reserved. No part of this publication may be reproduced,
stored in a retrieval system, or transmitted, in any form or by any means,
electronic, mechanical, photocopying, recording, or otherwise,
without the prior permission of Elizabeth Lymer or Mindworks Publishing.

http://www.mindworksbooks.com

With the name of Allah;
All thanks and praise are for Allah

For Aziem – EL

Islamic Nursery Rhymes

The Muslims Round The World

Oh, the Muslims round the world,
We pray five times a day;
We stand, we bow, prostrate, and kneel,
And we turn our heads each way.
And when we stand we are up,
And when we prostrate we are down,
And when we bow we're halfway up –
That's neither up nor down.

(Sing to tune of *The Grand Old Duke of York*)

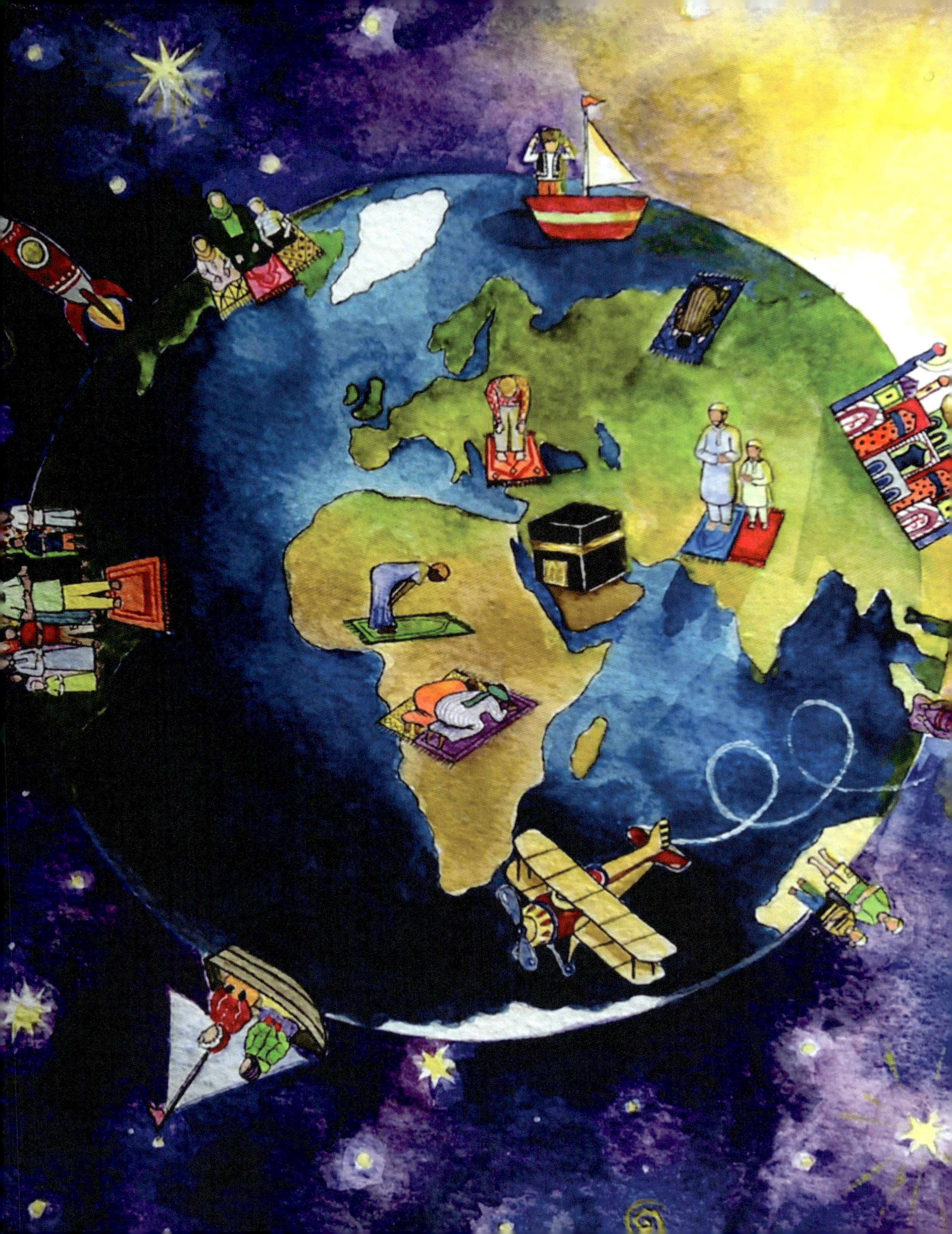

Assalaam 'Alaykum

(Sing to tune of *Oranges and Lemons*)

Assalaam 'alaykum,
Says the Masjid
in Leyton.
Wa 'alaykum salaam,
Says the Masjid
in East Ham.

When will Salah be?
Says the Masjid
in Hackney.
The sun will tell,
Says the Mosque
in Shadwell.

Who do we name?
Says the Mosque
on Brick Lane.
We worship Allah,
Says the Mosque
in Poplar.

Here's the Adhan
to call us to prayer.

Here's the Iqama,
so hurry, be there!

Laa ilaaha ilallah!

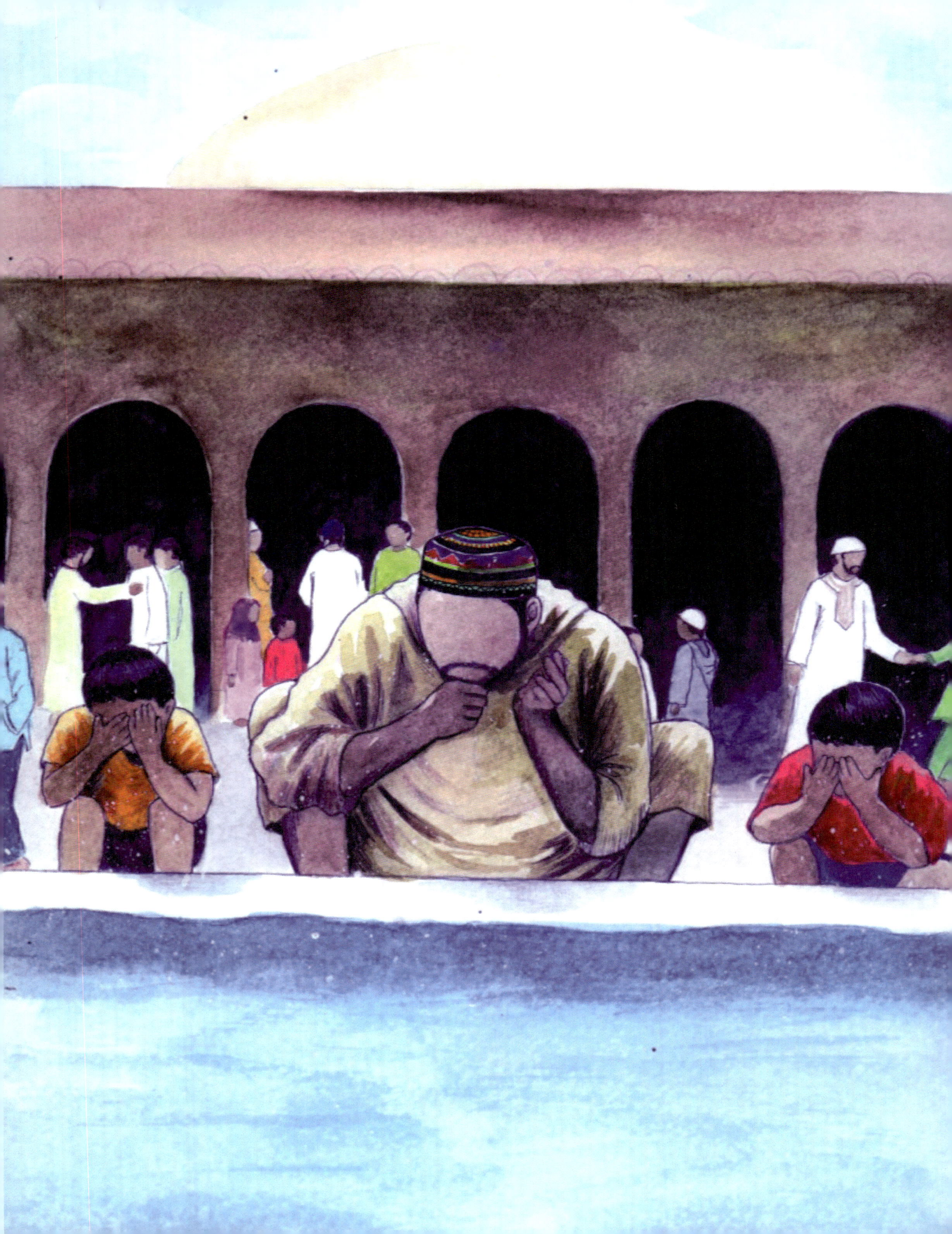

Wudu'

(Sing to tune of *Pop Goes The Weasel*)

Make intention, bismillah,
ready for Wudu'-oo,
ablution for Salah with care,
here's what to do-oo.
Wash your hands,
your mouth,
your nose,
your face,
your arms
to the elbows,
head, ears, feet,
the order goes,
even between toes.

SUBHAN-ALLAH!
ALHAMDULILLAH PRAISE BE TO ALLAH
GLORY BE TO ALLAH!

Worship Allah There

(Say to tune of *Shoe A Little Horse*)

Worship Allah there;
worship Allah here;

in worship Allah's always
near, near, near.

Feel that Allah's there;
feel that Allah's here;

be grateful Allah's always
near, near, near.

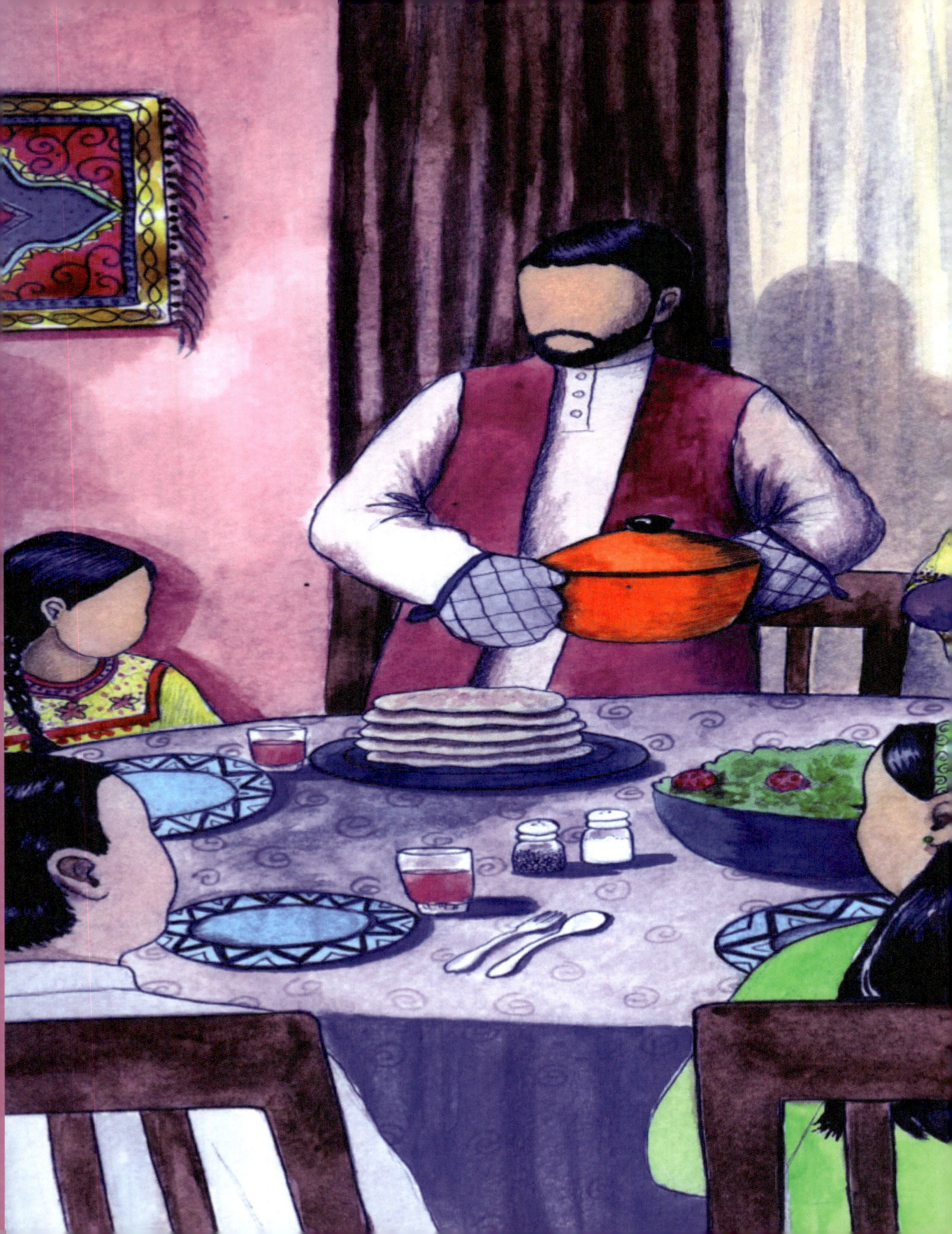

We Gather Altogether

(Sing to tune of *Miss Polly Had A Dolly*)

We gather altogether
when we eat, eat, eat.
Also, sometimes with neighbours
from our street, street, street.

A time for food,
but so much more besides,
for each meal helps us hold
stronger family ties.

Allah grants us food and drink
to share, share, share,
and there's always enough
when we are fair, fair, fair.

We thank Allah
and ask for His blessings,
for He's the Provider
of all things, things, things.

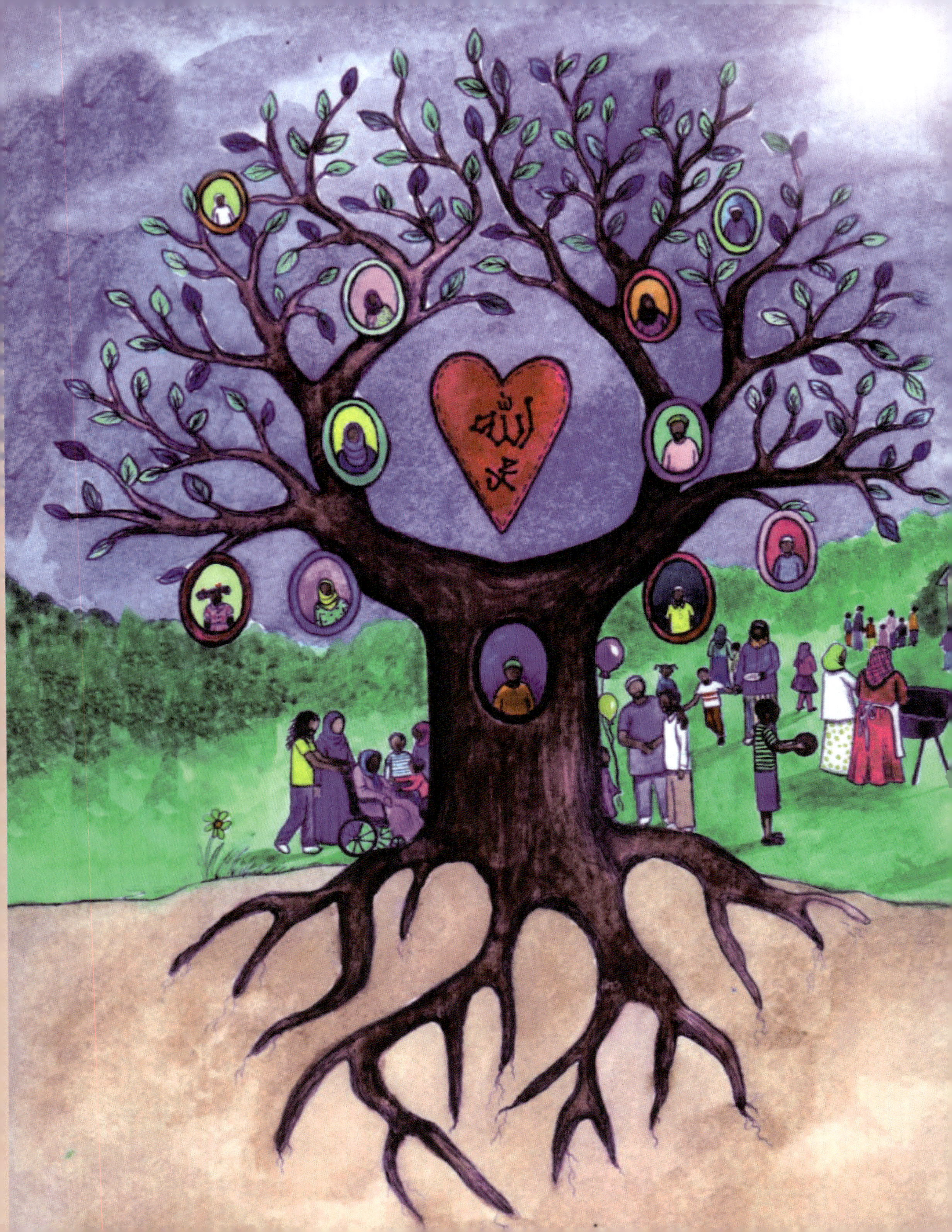
الله

Bond, Bond, With All Your Kin

Bond, bond, with all your kin,
Stick together through everything,
Avoid what's wrong,
keep good and strong,
And love each other
all along.

(Sing to tune of *Tom Tom The Piper's Son*)

Muhammad, Peace Be Upon Him

(Sing to tune of *Aiken Drum*)

There was a man lived long ago,
long ago, long ago,
There was a man lived long ago,
And Muhammad was his name.

Chorus
When we say his name we pray too,
we pray too, we pray too,
when we say his name we pray too,
for peace upon his name.

And he was a prophet of Allah,
of Allah, of Allah,
and he was a prophet of Allah,
and Muhammad was his name.

And his way was made of good manners,
good manners, good manners,
and his way was made of good manners,
and Muhammad was his name.

And his Sunnah way we follow,
we follow, we follow,
and his Sunnah way we follow,
and Muhammad was his name.

بِسْمِ اللهِ الرَّحْمٰنِ الرَّحِيْمِ

I ♥ MUHAMMAD

الله رسول محمد

Helpful Hannah

Helpful Hannah is well mannered,
Treating all with care,
By her manner, all know Hannah
To be kind and fair.
Why such manner, Helpful Hannah?
Don't you tire or sorrow?
Says Helpful Hannah, it's the Sunnah
For Allah I follow.

(Sing to tune of *Simple Simon*)

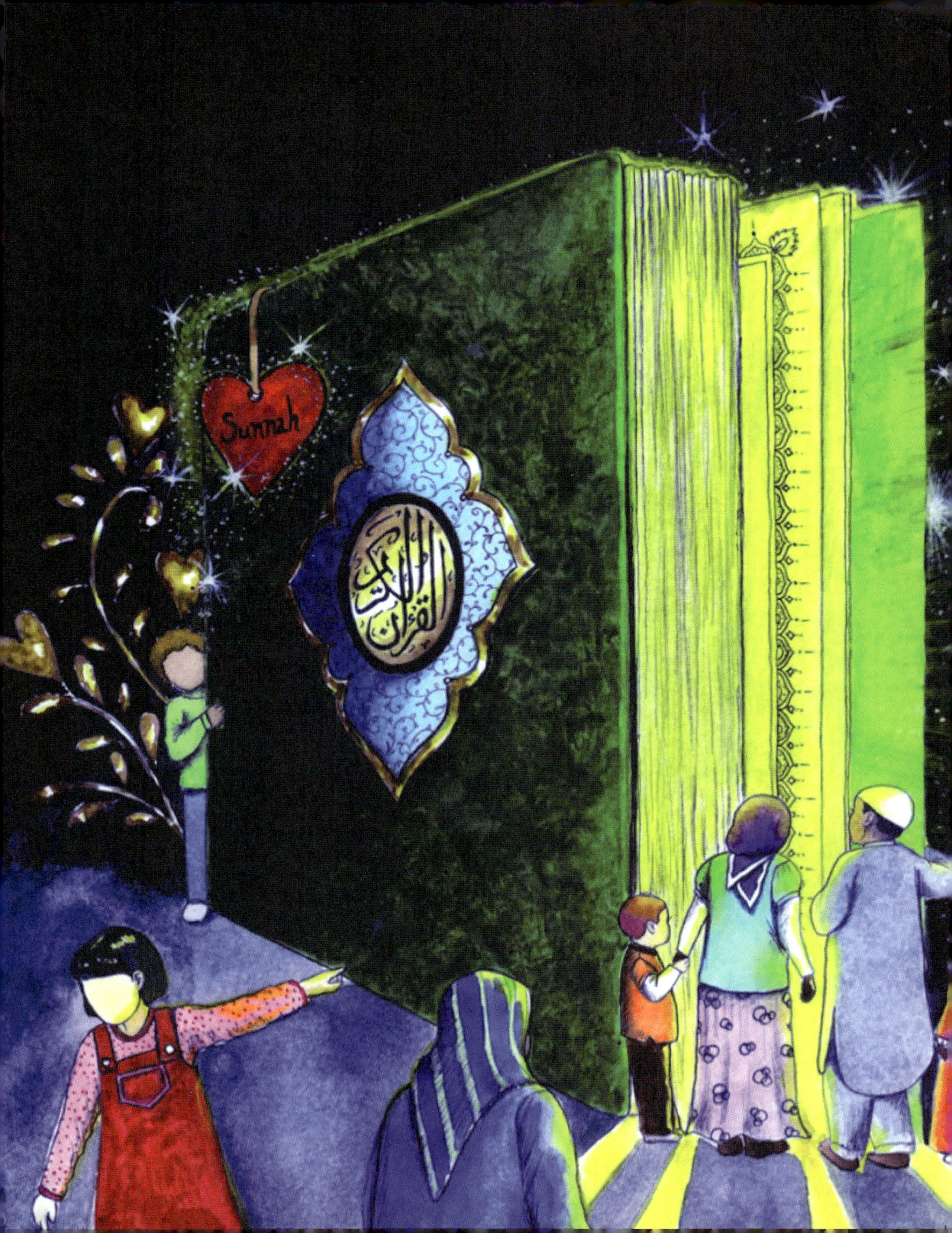
Sunnah
القرآن الكريم

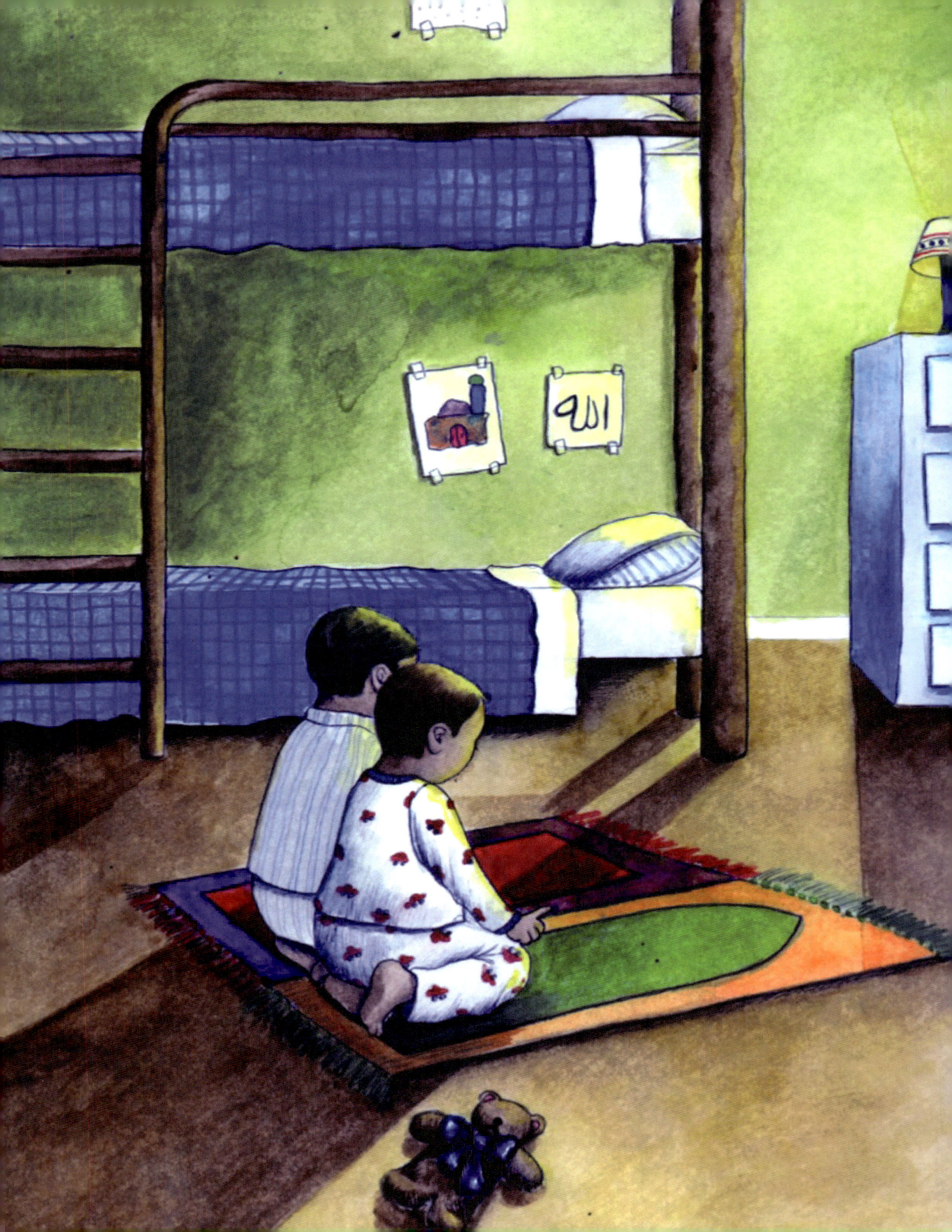

After 'Isha' We Can Sleep

After 'Isha' we can sleep,
We can sleep, we can sleep,
After 'Isha' we can sleep,
Bismillah.

Make wudu' and go to bed,
Go to bed, go to bed,
Make wudu' and go to bed,
Bismillah.

Read Qur'an and then lie down,
Then lie down, then lie down,
Read Qur'an and then lie down,
Bismillah.

Make dua' and close our eyes,
Close our eyes, close our eyes,
Make dua' and close our eyes,
Bismillah.

Soundly sleep in peace all night,
Peace all night, peace all night,
Soundly sleep in peace all night,
Bismillah.

(Sing to tune of *London Bridge Is Falling Down*)

The Five Prayer Times

(Sing to tune of *The Cock Crows*)

The first prayer of the day

Is long before sunrise,

The next is gone noon,

Those on time are wise.

So bow and prostrate,

Stand, kneel and rise,

The way of this worship

Is worthy and wise.

The third prayer time starts

With late afternoon sky,

The fourth at sunset,

The fifth in the night.

So bow and prostrate,

Stand, kneel and rise,

The way of this worship

Is worthy and wise.

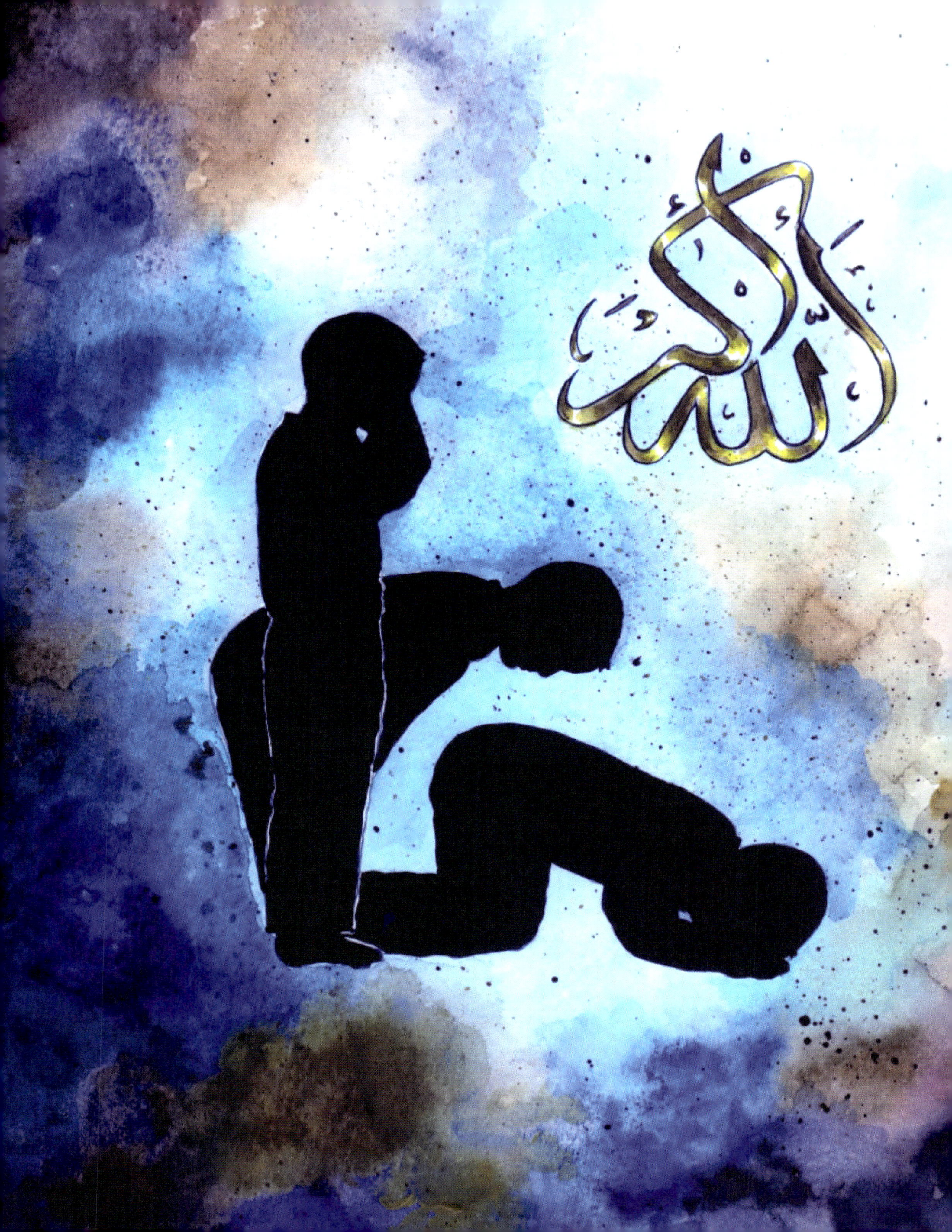
الله أكبر

Tired Muslims

(Sing to tune of *Little Boy Blue*)

Tired Muslims, lay down on your right,
Put trust in Allah for protection all night,

Remember Allah in your hearts and your heads,

And let yourselves rest now you're in bed.

Printed in Great Britain
by Amazon